Incidents in the Life of
JOSEPH GRIMALDI

INCIDENTS
IN THE LIFE OF
JOSEPH
GRIMALDI

By Giles Neville

Paintings by Patricia Neville

JONATHAN CAPE
THIRTY BEDFORD SQUARE LONDON

First published 1980
Copyright © 1980 by Giles Neville
Illustrations copyright © 1980 by Patricia Neville
Jonathan Cape Ltd, 30 Bedford Square, London WC1

British Library Cataloguing in Publication Data

Neville, Giles
Incidents in the life of Joseph Grimaldi.
1. Grimaldi, Joseph   2. Clowns – Great
Britain – Biography
I. Title
791.3'3'0924   GV1811.G7
ISBN 0 224 01869 8

Patricia Neville's original works of art are exhibited
exclusively by Portal Gallery Ltd, London, England.

Conditions of sale

Printed in Italy by New Interlitho, SpA, Milan

Introduction

JOSEPH GRIMALDI was possibly the funniest and certainly the most celebrated comic actor and pantomime artist that the British stage has ever known. Loved by the London mob and patronised by the aristocracy, befriended by Byron and praised by the essayist Hazlitt, Grimaldi's popularity was such that in his heyday at the beginning of the nineteenth century he was able to fill the vast old Covent Garden Theatre to capacity for ninety-two successive performances.

Although he appeared almost exclusively in pantomimes, Grimaldi did not only take to the stage at Christmas, nor did his audiences consist principally of children. For in those days pantomimes were performed all the year round (often as the second half of a sort of theatrical 'double-bill'), and attended and enjoyed by people from all age groups and classes.

The pantomimes themselves used to revolve round the humorous escapades of a number of stock characters, the most important of whom were Pantaloon, Harlequin, Clown and Columbine, and it was customary for a pantomimist to specialise in one or other of these roles. Thus Grimaldi was best known for playing Clown, and indeed so closely was he associated with this part, a part which he had in fact been largely responsible for creating, that the theatre-going public's affectionate name for him, 'Joey', came in the course of time to be a synonym for a Clown.

'Joey' Grimaldi was born illegitimately in London on the 18th December 1778. His father was a comic pantomimist and dancing instructor who, though his Christian name was Giuseppe, was commonly known as Signor Grimaldi, and his mother, Mrs. Rebecca Brooker, was a dancer at the Drury Lane Theatre. While little is known about the latter, quite a lot has come down to us concerning Signor Grimaldi, who was born in Italy and appears to have arrived in England as a middle-aged man some time towards the end of the 1750s. Thus by the time of Joseph's birth he was already old, sixty-five to be exact, and, by all accounts, something of an eccentric. As a husband and a parent he had, to say the least, his short-comings, for he was tyrannical, a notorious womaniser, and subjected Joseph to frequent thrashings. He was also morbid and superstitious: a side of his personality that manifested itself in a variety of peculiar obsessions and phobias, one of which was a fear of being buried alive.

5

This preyed upon his mind to such an extent that he stipulated in his will that his head was to be severed from his body prior to his burial. His wish was duly granted, and the gruesome operation actually carried out in front of several witnesses.

As a performer Signor Grimaldi was popular with audiences and critics alike—though some of his jokes and antics occasionally upset the more prudish theatre-goers. And by the time of his death in 1788 he was so well known that it probably was not until a good many years afterwards that Joseph—who ultimately became much more famous than he ever was—ceased to be referred to as the *son* of Grimaldi.

Since both Joseph's parents were employed in the theatre it was—given the age in which he was born—virtually inevitable that he would follow their example and make the stage his profession: not that he originally had much say in the matter, as he was less than three years old when, on Easter Monday 1781, he made his début. Shortly afterwards he was engaged, through Signor Grimaldi's influence, on a regular basis at both Sadler's Wells and Drury Lane, and from then until his premature retirement forty-odd years later, the theatre was indisputably the centre of his life: it was there as a child that he played; there that he founded the majority of his friendships; there that he met and courted his two wives; and there in the green-rooms that he encountered many of the best known society figures of his day.

First and foremost, however, the theatre was where Joseph made his living. To begin with, of course, his weekly wages were low, no more than a few shillings; but by 1789 he was being paid over £1 at Drury Lane, though less at Sadler's Wells; and by 1802 he was receiving around £4 and £6 at Drury Lane and Sadler's Wells, respectively. (An agricultural labourer at the turn of the century could not hope to earn more than £8 *a year*.) During the last twenty years or so of his career wages represented but a part of Joseph's income, perhaps as much as half of his money accruing from benefit nights and provincial tours. Thus when he played at Rochester for two nights in 1801 (his first provincial engagement), he collected in all £160—forty times what he made in a week at Drury Lane. However, he was a spendthrift and, with the help of his second wife, who had 'a love of dress which almost amounted to a mania', usually went through his money as quickly as he earned it.

In 1800, at the age of twenty-one, Grimaldi landed his first leading part in a pantomime, playing one of two Clowns in a production called *Peter Wilkins: or The Flying World*. But his rise to fame was gradual rather than meteoric, and he did not win universal acclaim until Christmas 1806, when the legendary pantomime *Mother Goose* opened at Covent Garden—which theatre he had joined a few months earlier, having fallen out with the manager at Drury Lane. *Mother Goose* was an unprecedented success—by the time it closed in June the following year it had reputedly made Covent Garden a profit of more than £20,000; and its popularity was almost wholly attributable to Grimaldi. Thereafter he was in a class of his own. He was quite simply the funniest living pantomimist: so funny that George IV once burst his stays laughing at him; so funny that, on another occasion, he caused a deaf and dumb sailor to recover miraculously his powers of speech and hearing. It was indeed Grimaldi's abilities as a mime, the extraordinary expressiveness of his face and body, that above all else distinguished him from his contemporaries and gave him his unique power to make people laugh—and cry as well. His nose alone, we are told, was 'capable of exhibiting disdain, fear, anger, even joy'.

While the theatre was the centre of Grimaldi's life, he was nevertheless a shy and rather unworldly person who generally preferred the tranquillity of his home and the company of his wife to the excitement and stimulation of society. His first wife, whom he worshipped, was Maria Hughes. She died less than two years after their marriage, in 1800. Although his feelings for his second wife, Mary Bristow, were perhaps not as strong, they lived together happily enough for over thirty years, and it was she who, in 1802, gave birth to his only child, Joseph Samuel. Despite the fact that Grimaldi must have inherited some characteristics from his none-too-blameless father, by and large Signor Grimaldi's most conspicuous faults corresponded to his virtues. Thus whereas 'Old Grim' was domineering, Joseph was considerate; whereas the former was a philanderer, the latter was faithful to both his wives; and whereas Joseph was treated harshly by Signor Grimaldi, he brought up his own son with love and kindness.

After Grimaldi retired from the stage in 1823—not, as might be supposed, because his popularity had waned, but due to ill-health—the remainder of his life was far from happy. His health did not improve, he worried about money, and the behaviour of his son, who died in 1832 after ruining a promising stage career through his drunkenness, caused him great distress. Then, in 1834 or 1835, his wife Mary died. Not long afterwards he began writing his autobiography, 'his chief occupation and amusement', which he completed in December 1836. In his conclusion he wrote: 'In my solitary hours—and in spite of all the kindness of my friends I have many of them—my thoughts often dwell upon the past: and there is one circumstance which always affords me unmitigated satisfaction; it is simply that I cannot recollect one single instance in which I have intentionally wronged man, woman, or child, and this gives me great satisfaction and comfort.'

He died on the night of the 31st May 1837.

Signor Grimaldi and the Gordon Riots

IN 1780, when Joseph Grimaldi's father, Signor Grimaldi, was living in Little Russell Street in London, the Gordon Riots took place. Mobs surged through the streets attacking all those that they took to be Papists (as Catholics were then disparagingly called); and because of the arbitrariness of the violence, which was directed against property as well as individuals, all but the most foolhardy house-holders attempted to safeguard their homes and families by chalking the words 'No Popery!' on their doors.

It was a dangerous time, and especially dangerous for foreigners: for as the mobs were dimly aware that Catholicism was rife on the other side of the Channel, to be known by a title such as Signor or Monsieur was to be suspected of Popery. However, Signor Grimaldi, despite the fact that his Italian origins were widely known, and moreover hardly disguised by his swarthy complexion and broken English, did not inscribe his door with the usual 'No Popery!' Instead, perhaps because he was reluctant to renounce the faith of his forefathers, he announced in large characters on the outside of his house that he had 'No Religion At All'.

How much of a risk Signor Grimaldi was taking by so doing, it is im-possible to say in retrospect. But since neither he nor his house was attacked during the disturbances, it can be assumed that any rioters who chanced to catch sight of his inscription found it humorous rather than provocative.

*   *   *

While the above is what one might call the official account of Signor Grimaldi's behaviour during the Gordon Riots (in as much as it is the one set down by Joseph Grimaldi in his memoirs), another version of the story was recorded by Henry Angelo, a pantomime artist who was taught dancing by Signor Grimaldi.

In this version Signor Grimaldi refused—or simply did not bother—to write the customary slogan on the outside of the building in which he was living. As a consequence his home was one day besieged by an angry mob, which had noticed the absence of any 'No Popery!' inscription, and, knowing that he was a foreigner, had taken this to be a sign that he was a Papist. The bolder spirits were on the point of storming the house when Signor Grimaldi, who had been listening inside, appeared at a second floor window. Undeterred by the abuse and rotten vegetables with which the crowd greeted his sudden appearance, he pushed open the window, stuck his head out, and declared in a loud voice: 'Genteelmen, in dis hose

dere be no religion at all.'

This announcement, and the ludicrous grimaces with which the wily old clown accompanied it, completely won over the rioters, who, before proceeding on their way, gave him three resounding cheers.

Signor Grimaldi and his Lambeth Garden

ONE morning, towards the end of a particularly harsh winter, Signor Grimaldi announced to his family that he intended purchasing 'a nice bitaground' — from which his common-law wife, Mrs. Brooker, understood that what he wished to buy was some land. And although, knowing how whimsical he was, she did not take his announcement too seriously, she nevertheless made a point of tapping him for the housekeeping before he went out.

No doubt she was subsequently glad that she had: for that evening he returned home overjoyed, having acquired a plot of land in Lambeth. It was, he admitted, 'no very big', and, like everywhere else in London, a foot deep in snow. But part of it was laid out as a garden, and he enthusiastically described what he imagined it would look like a few months thenceforward.

At breakfast the next day Signor Grimaldi was moody and irritable. It was not his career that troubled him (for he was being well received in London at the time): it was his little Lambeth garden. He simply could not wait to see his trees bearing fruit and his borders full of flowers — and spring, let alone summer, seemed an age away. How he cursed the 'Ingleesh' climate!

Later that same morning he was sitting disconsolately in his parlour, absent-mindedly toying with some pretty wax fruit that belonged to his wife, when suddenly he struck upon a marvellous idea: why, he need not wait until summer came, he would *make* summer come! Without further ado he despatched young Joseph to the shops, and, pocketing the fruit, rushed off to see his old friend the prop-master at Drury Lane. As soon as he had gathered together all that he needed for his purpose, he set out for Lambeth, accompanied by Joseph and his friend from the theatre.

They arrived at the plot of land, and using an extraordinary assortment of artificial fruit and flowers, immediately set about decorating the garden. Signor Grimaldi supervised everything; and as his fantastic idea began to take shape he grew more and more excited. At last they were finished. He made one final adjustment to the petals of a flower, stepped back a few paces to admire their work, and then, being Italian, burst unashamedly into tears of pleasure. For it was a truly wonderful sight: above, apples, pears and plums, and even tangerines and peaches, fashioned out of wax or porcelain or papier mâché, depended from the hitherto barren branches of the staid English fruit trees; while below, dozens of paper and fabric flowers made little dots and splashes of bright colour against the white backdrop of the snow.

10

Joseph Grimaldi and the Dartford Blues

ESPITE the fact that young Joseph Grimaldi must have spent the majority of his waking hours working in the theatre, he still somehow found the time, and the energy, to cultivate a number of unusual hobbies. Designing mechanical stage effects was one of them; playing the fiddle another; but his chief passion—perhaps because it both combined elements of skill, luck and exercise, and had that special quality which is peculiar to activities that can only be pursued at certain times or seasons—was butterfly collecting. Whenever he could in the summer months, Joseph would roam the countryside around London equipped with a net and a bottle. And occasionally, if he heard from a fellow enthusiast that a rare or interesting species was to be found in another part of the country, he would venture farther afield.

Thus in June 1794, when he was fifteen years old, Joseph learnt that a rare butterfly, dubbed the Dartford Blue, was that month flourishing in the vicinity of the town in Kent from which it had derived its popular name. As this butterfly was not yet represented in his collection, he decided it merited a trip to Dartford; and accordingly he set out very early one Friday morning after appearing at Drury Lane.

He walked through the night to the town (a journey of about fifteen miles) and, arriving there at five o'clock as dawn was breaking, called on a friend of his named Brooks. He took a short nap, and after breakfasting with his friend, went off by himself to look for butterflies. Having netted one Dartford Blue, he returned to his friend's house at midday; and pleased but not satisfied with a single example, he arranged to see Brooks again the following morning. He then walked back to London, had tea and went to work at Drury Lane.

At the end of the pantomime he set out once more for Dartford. Excited as he was by the prospect of catching more of the prized butterflies, he covered the distance more rapidly than he had the previous night, reaching the town while it was still dark. He knocked up Brooks, again availed himself of his friend's hospitality, and as soon as it was light enough for him to do so, resumed his search.

Luck was on his side that morning, for he discovered a copse that harboured an abundance of butterflies, and at the end of a few hours he had succeeded in catching no less than forty-eight Dartford Blues. Delighted by both the number and the beauty of his specimens, he spent the remainder of the morning carefully arranging them in a wooden display case which he had brought with him. This delicate task so absorbed

him that he forgot to keep track of the time; and when he had finally done with his pins and labels he found to his dismay that it was already half past two. Fearful lest he should be late for the evening performance at Drury Lane, he bid Brooks a hasty farewell and hurried off to London.

By running most of the way and foregoing his tea, he managed to reach the theatre before the curtain rose. He changed into his costume with great alacrity, and notwithstanding his hunger and growing fatigue performed his part as faultlessly as ever.

At some point in the course of the evening he happened to pass in a backstage corridor the famous Mrs. Jordan, an actress much acclaimed for her beauty and charm, who was then attached to the theatre's company. They exchanged smiles as they went by; and then, as Mrs. Jordan's curiosity had been aroused by the wooden box she had noticed Joseph clutching protectively to his chest, she stopped abruptly, causing her retinue of admirers to stumble into one another, and called him back.

'Whatever have you got in that case, Joseph?' she enquired kindly.

Joseph gazed up at her and blushed, overawed by the interest the great lady was taking in *him*, one of the youngest and humblest members of the cast. After a few seconds, however, he managed to blurt out, ''Flies, Ma'am.'

At first Mrs. Jordan misunderstood his reply, and as he slipped back the lid of the box to show her his treasures, she backed away, half expecting him to release a cloud of nasty houseflies.

'Oh—you mean *butter*flies!' she exclaimed with relief when she saw the contents of the case. She looked at them more closely and added, 'Ooh! Aren't they *beautiful*!'

'Beautiful, beautiful,' echoed her admirers (who always agreed with her), even though none of them could actually see into the box from where they were standing.

Mrs. Jordan was enchanted by the young lepidopterist. She asked him where and how he had caught the insects, and whether he had mounted them himself; and she listened attentively to his answers—though she begged him not to dwell on the details of the killing jar. After a few minutes the actress was summoned to the wings to await her cue, and so, to the regret of both parties, they had to break off their conversation. But before they separated she led Joseph to understand that she would love to have a frame of the pretty blue butterflies—if ever he should happen to have one he could spare.

It seemed to Joseph, when Mrs. Jordan and her train had gone, that he had never met a sweeter, kinder lady; and he resolved there and then to make, on her behalf, one last trip to Dartford that night. For although by this time he was almost dropping with tiredness, he was afraid that if

14

he delayed the expedition he might not find the number of butterflies necessary for a display worthy of his new idol. Besides, he told himself, as the next day was Sunday, he would be able to catch up with his sleep the following evening.

Thus for a third time Joseph quit London for Kent. But as we have already twice followed him on this journey, there can be few who would be interested to know at what time he left, or at what time he arrived, and whether he again roused Brooks, or whether, as it was the Sabbath, he refrained from disturbing him. Of this final journey, then, it is only necessary to record that he revisited the copse, that it was as well stocked with Dartford Blues as it had been the day before, and that he caught as many of them as he needed without any difficulty.

On the Monday evening, Joseph, having benefited from a full night's sleep, turned up as usual at Drury Lane. But before attending to his own affairs he went straight to Mrs. Jordan's dressing-room, and there shyly presented her with, not one, but two cases of Dartford Blues. The charming actress, who, it must be confessed, sometimes wearied of the *cadeaux* that were continually being pressed upon her by admirers and suitors, was thrilled with his offering, and especially touched by the great pains he had evidently taken to arrange the butterflies in a pleasing and original design.

'Joseph,' she said after she had thanked and kissed him many times, forgetting in her excitement that, unlike grown men, boys are not fond of kisses, 'is this really all your own work?'

And Joseph, who felt that he had been more handsomely rewarded by the lovely actress's praise and pleasure than he would have done had he been given a purse of golden guineas, nodded his head proudly.

If his reward that evening exceeded a purse of guineas, then a few days later it could not have been matched by a veritable chest of them. For he heard from Mrs. Jordan that she had shown his cases of Dartford Blues to no less a personage than His Royal Highness the Duke of Clarence (who was at that time her 'protector'), and that the future King William IV had pronounced them at least as good as, if not superior to, the best displays he had ever seen.

15

The Pentonville Robbers

OR SOME years prior to his first marriage in 1799, Joseph Grimaldi resided with his mother, Mrs. Brooker, in a house in Penton Place, North London. During part of that time the district in which they lived, Pentonville, was terrorised by a notorious gang of thieves known, appropriately enough, as the 'Pentonville Robbers'. By the summer of 1797, when Joseph and his mother happened to be sharing their house with a couple named Lewis, who were also connected with the theatre, the gang had all been captured and either hanged or transported—all, that is, save its two most desperate members.

These two cut-throats had heard exaggerated accounts of young Grimaldi's wealth, and observing that the house in Penton Place was often empty (all four occupants being engaged that summer at Sadler's Wells), they resolved to raid it.

A drunken stage-hand provided them with a useful tip: on such-and-such a date the whole Sadler's Wells cast would have to attend a night rehearsal at the theatre.

However, at the last moment the rehearsal was cancelled—to the great relief of the cast, who had been expecting to be kept up until at least four in the morning; and thus Grimaldi and the other members of the household, accompanied by two friends, returned home early, disturbing the thieves as they were escaping with their valuables. A light was struck, a candle lit, and the whole house, not excepting the cupboards, thoroughly searched by the menfolk. As soon as it had been established that the thieves had fled, Grimaldi seized—from its place above the mantelshelf—the weapon that was closest to hand, namely a large and ancient broadsword, and followed by a Mr. King with a cudgel, rushed out through the back door into the garden.

Seeing no sign of the robbers, Grimaldi left Mr. King bravely lunging at shadows by the vegetable patch and climbed up on to the garden wall to obtain a better view.

'Is that you?' hissed someone from the middle of a bush in the neighbouring garden. One of the burglars had mistaken Grimaldi for his accomplice.

'Yes—it's me,' Grimaldi hissed back. And leaping down from the wall, he struck the bush a great blow with the broadsword. With a scream and an oath and a shower of leaves the villain broke cover and made off into the night.

The Clown rushed to the end of the garden, jumped over into the pasture that lay beyond, and, with the intention of heading the robber off, began running along its edge. But in his haste he failed to notice the dark form that lay across his path ... suddenly he found himself somersaulting through the air, having tripped over the body of a sleeping cow. Only his acrobatic training saved him from impaling himself on the enormous sword. The startled animal stumbled wearily to its feet and stood staring reproachfully at Grimaldi, who, winded by his fall, lay prostrate on the dewy ground.

After a minute or so he picked himself up, shooed the cow away, retrieved his weapon, and deciding that further pursuit was useless, turned dispiritedly homewards.

Fortunately the household's valuables were later found where the thieves had dumped them, in the field at the end of the garden; and the only person who suffered any loss as a result of the burglary was Grimaldi, whose butterfly collection—which by that time consisted of upwards of four thousand specimens—had been wantonly destroyed. This caused him such distress that he subsequently sold or gave away his nets and what little remained of the collection, and he never afterwards had the heart to resume what had hitherto been his favourite hobby.

Although nothing could have rendered the loss Grimaldi had sustained any easier to bear, he at least had the satisfaction of seeing the men who had perpetrated the outrage brought to justice. For the two thieves, in an effort to retrieve the loot they had abandoned, made two further attempts at burgling Grimaldi's house. After their second attempt Grimaldi prudently sought the assistance of the law. On their third attempt they were tricked and trapped by a resourceful constable named Trott; and after being tried and convicted they were sent to join such of their old comrades as had escaped the drop, in Australia.

Old Lucas

ARLY one morning in spring 1798, Joseph Grimaldi set out from Penton Place to walk to Sadler's Wells, where he had a business appointment. As it did not happen to be raining that day, and as he was rather pressed for time, he decided to take a shortcut across Sadler's Wells Fields—a large expanse of unenclosed wasteland that lay between his home and the theatre. He had scarcely closed the front door, however, before he became aware that something extraordinary was taking place in the neighbourhood. At first he was puzzled to see a number of disreputable local characters—men not normally known for their love of fresh air and exercise—scurrying excitedly past his garden gate towards Sadler's Wells Fields. Then, as he approached the edge of the common, he began to hear the sound of distant shrieks and yells. Finally, in the middle of Sadler's Wells Fields, he discovered the source of all the noise and excitement: a huge, unruly mob was engaged in baiting a stray ox.

Disgusted by the cruelty of the sport and finding his path blocked, he halted a little way off from the crowd and tried to make up his mind whether it was worth turning back and taking the longer, but under the circumstances safer, route to the theatre via the Angel at Islington. He stood irresolute for a few minutes until a stranger, a young gentleman, tapped him on the arm, and, without introducing himself, enquired if he was Joseph Grimaldi. Grimaldi was surprised by the youth's directness, but nevertheless replied in the affirmative, and then asked him who he was and what it was that he wanted.

'Never mind who I am, sir. And I want nothing from you. But I thought I should warn you that you are the object of considerable interest to that gentleman over there.' So saying, the youth pointed out an unpleasant-looking individual at the centre of a knot of men loitering close by, whom Grimaldi recognised—by his spectacles—to be the parish constable, Lucas; or Old Lucas, as he was generally called. The epithet, however, was misleading: for it did not describe his age, nor had it been bestowed upon him (as is sometimes the case) because he inspired affection in his fellow men. Old Lucas was, in fact, a cunning, corrupt, middle-aged man, who—for the sake of the 'expenses' he could claim upon obtaining a conviction—specialised in charging wholly innocent people with crimes that they had not committed.

Grimaldi was therefore perturbed by the stranger's intelligence and anxiously asked him whether he might not have been mistaken. But the young gentleman had not been mistaken: he had even overheard Old

Lucas boasting to his companions that he could 'lay hold of Grimaldi' whenever he wanted to.

On hearing this Grimaldi grew very frightened, as he could only conclude that Old Lucas was planning to bring some false charge against him. Determined, however, that the scheming constable was not going to lay hold of him there and then, he thanked the young gentleman for his information, and, as the crowd looked just as dangerous and impenetrable as it had a few minutes before, rushed off in the direction of the Angel.

The business that Grimaldi had to attend to at the theatre was so absorbing that he forgot all about Old Lucas and his machinations until later that day, when a remark that was made in the dressing-rooms while he and the other members of the Sadler's Wells cast were preparing themselves for the evening pantomime served to remind him of the events of the morning. Suddenly feeling in need of a little friendly advice and sympathy, he turned to his fellow actors.

But for once Grimaldi misjudged his audience; for his colleagues were in a playful, bantering mood that evening, and, disregarding his appeal for advice and sympathy, they responded to his troubles with perverse jocularity. Old Lucas, they all agreed, was as honest and upright an official as one could ever hope to find—a credit to the parish; and if *he* had reason to suspect *Grimaldi*—a mere pantomimist with a foreign-sounding name— of some crime or other, why that was enough for them! Grimaldi's fellow actors disagreed, however, when it came to speculating about the nature of the crime he had committed. Dubois, a well-known clown, suggested that Grimaldi—who had already earned a name for the way he could filch a ham or a string of sausages on the stage—had been abusing his talents and dipping into the pockets of the local inhabitants. Another asserted, for some reason, that he had been forging coins; while a third claimed that he was, in fact, the man responsible for a terrible murder which had been reported in the newspapers a few weeks before. The clamour that ensued reached its climax when one of the cast leapt up on a table and, cupping his hands to his mouth, declared that they had underestimated Grimaldi's capacity for wickedness: he was not guilty of just one or other of the crimes suggested that evening, he was guilty of *all* of them!

The roars of laughter with which this announcement was greeted were abruptly stifled, however, when the dressing-room door banged open and a messenger mechanically announced that Mr. Grimaldi was wanted by someone at the stage-door. Grimaldi, who had been sitting silent all this time, looking rather bewildered, stood up and asked who it was that wished to see him. On learning that it was Old Lucas he collapsed, ashen-faced, on to his chair. Immediately the atmosphere in the room changed. Grimaldi's friends gathered round him with words of comfort and encouragement; and Dubois, who was particularly attached to him, expressed the feelings of all when he said, 'Joe, m'boy, we've had a bit of fun here tonight, and you were the butt. We likes a lark—it's in our nature—and none of us bears you any malice. But as there's one out there that does' (he jabbed his thumb in the direction of the stage-door) 'we'll all go with you now and stand by you, and show ourselves to be your loyal friends.' Having said this he helped Grimaldi to his feet, put his arm round his shoulders, and they all trooped off to confront Old Lucas.

They met the constable at the top of the steps that led up to the stage-door. Once they had all assembled around him, Old Lucas shook his head grimly and in a gesture of unconcern took off his glasses and began polishing them with an unspeakably filthy rag that he had extracted from one of his pockets.

'If I had wanted to see,' he said in a quiet voice, looking round at the actors, 'the whole company,' he paused; 'I would have arst to see,' he continued in a louder voice, 'the *whole* company.' He paused again. 'But I never arst to see the whole company,' he shouted, 'I arst to see Mussyare Grimaldi!'

Undaunted by the constable, Dubois stepped forward. 'Bawling won't increase your authority with us, Old Lucas. We're here as his friends, an' there's no rules against that. Now say what you've come to say to him in front of all of us before we throw you in the river.' The river being the

23

New River, which in those days flowed past Sadler's Wells.

Old Lucas thrust his spectacles back on his nose and peered fiercely first at Dubois, and then over the latter's shoulder at Grimaldi.

'Joseph Grimaldi,' he said, 'I'm here to charge you and take you into custody for the crime of harassing, and inciting others to harass, a stray ox on Sadler's Wells Fields, not twelve hours ago, to the detriment of the said ox's reason and the danger of His Majesty's subjects.'

'Liar!' cried out Grimaldi.

'*Liar*?' The constable repeated the word in disbelief. '*You* dare to call *me* a liar? You'd better come with me now, Grimaldi, before I think of a few extra charges to add to the one of ox-baiting.'

'Where's your warrant, Lucas?' demanded Dubois, who knew something of the law.

'I have witnesses,' replied Old Lucas, avoiding the question.

'The warrant, Lucas!' the actors all shouted together, advancing angrily on the constable.

Fearing that they might execute Dubois' threat, Lucas hastily retreated to the bottom of the steps, where he reluctantly admitted that he had no warrant.

'But,' he growled, 'that makes no odds. The charge stands.' And then, adopting a more placatory tone, he added, 'However, under these—ahem—unusual circumstances, I'm willing to allow Grimaldi to remain at liberty—on the condition that he undertakes to present himself before Mr. Blamire, the magistrate, at Hatton Garden Police Office tomorrow morning at eleven o'clock.'

Grimaldi gave his word, and Old Lucas turned to go. But the altercation had attracted a large group of those types who invariably gather whenever there is a street accident or an argument, or anything out of the ordinary worth gaping at, and on trying to leave, the unpopular constable found himself jostled by a hooting, jeering mass of people. Hurling threats at those whom he recognised, he pushed his way roughly through the crowd and made off amidst a hail of rotten apples, mud, and anything else the crowd could lay their hands on.

The next day, shortly before eleven o'clock, Grimaldi and most of the cast from Sadler's Wells congregated in the ante-room at Hatton Garden Office. While his supporters stood around whispering among themselves, Grimaldi nervously tapped a foot in time to the ticking of the ante-room clock and fiddled with his waistcoat buttons. Several minutes passed. Then, just as the clock was striking the hour, the door from the street swung open, and Grimaldi visibly relaxed. For in stepped the young gentleman who had accosted him on the common. Grimaldi had managed to establish his identity late the night before, and had sent him a note urging him to come and testify on his behalf. But as he had received no reply, he had not known whether the young man would be either able or willing to attend. Grimaldi darted forward and embraced the stranger like his oldest friend.

A moment later a functionary appeared and ushered Grimaldi, his supporters and his only witness into the court room. Old Lucas and his cronies were already seated on the left of Mr. Blamire with suitably respectful expressions on their faces, and once Grimaldi and his friends had installed themselves on the opposite side of the room, the magistrate proceeded to hear the case. He listened carefully to everything that was said, made a few notes, and warned Dubois that he would be ejected if he persisted in heckling the prosecution witnesses.

At last Mr. Blamire announced his decision. He told the court that although he had been impressed by, and felt inclined to believe, the defendant and his witness (whom he understood came from a very good family), he had to bear in mind that a parish constable had testified, under oath, to having seen, with his 'own eyes', Grimaldi commit the offence of which he stood accused. A verdict which wholly exonerated the defendant, he went on, would suggest that the officer had committed perjury—'an ugly word which, I am sorry to say, has already been bandied about my court this morning.' He had decided therefore to fine Mr. Grimaldi a sum that he could easily afford—five shillings—and to order him to be discharged.

The Grimaldi party greeted this verdict with cheers; and as soon as their hero had paid the fine—plus a shilling for his discharge—to the Clerk of the Court, they carried him off on their shoulders to the King of Prussia, a nearby public house.

A first round of drinks having been purchased and consumed, they were all eagerly discussing the two issues that were uppermost in their minds, namely, the villainies of Old Lucas and who should buy the next round—when in burst one of their number with the news that the constable himself was at that moment approaching the public house.

A few seconds later Lucas entered the bar. To everybody's astonishment he strode straight up to Grimaldi and demanded in a loud voice that he hand over the fine which he had left the court without paying, adding that if he did not do so immediately he would have no option but to arrest him. Grimaldi could hardly believe what he heard, and having had as much of Old Lucas as he could take, he clenched his fists and, without bothering to protest that he had already paid his six shillings, informed the constable that if he did not quit the tavern that instant he would have cause to regret it.

'Won't cough up, eh? Threaten me, eh?' roared Old Lucas, lunging forward and pulling Grimaldi from his stool.

There was a sound of ripping cotton, a cry of 'I warned you!' from Grimaldi, and Old Lucas suddenly reeled backwards, clutching his nose with one hand and the Clown's shirt collar in the other. The constable recovered himself, wiped his bloody nose, straightened his spectacles, and then unsheathing his truncheon advanced again upon Grimaldi. But before he had had a chance to bring his weapon to bear, a man dashed between them waving a silver tipstaff and crying, 'Enough, gentlemen, enough!' At the sight of the tipstaff (which served to indicate that the bearer was an officer of the law), Old Lucas lowered his truncheon and Grimaldi replaced the stool he had picked up in order to defend himself. Laying hold of the two panting men, the officer, with the air of one accustomed to exercising authority, ordered them to return with him to Mr. Blamire's court—whither they went, followed of course by Grimaldi's friends.

Once they had all assembled in the court, the officer explained how he had witnessed the two men, whose names he had since learnt were Grimaldi and Lucas, brawling in the Commercial Bar of a local tavern. He then went on to describe what had taken place with such accuracy and impartiality that when the magistrate turned to Grimaldi and Lucas and asked them if they had anything to say, neither of them was able to deny, or add to, any part of the officer's account; although Lucas took the opportunity to make a great show of nursing his squashed nose, whining, 'Bloodied and broken, y'r Honour. Bloodied and broken.'

But if the constable had hoped to win Mr. Blamire's sympathy, he was disappointed. For the magistrate merely looked at his injury with a curious expression on his face (Dubois swore afterwards that he was grinning), and then asked the Clerk of the Court whether the fine had been paid. The Clerk confirmed that it had; and as Mr. Blamire (who was as fond of his lunch as any member of his profession) noticed that it was already past one o'clock, he delivered his verdict with uncharacteristic economy. He found Old Lucas guilty of trying to obtain money under false pretences and of provoking the fight which had occurred in the bar of the King of Prussia. For these offences he fined the constable five pounds—the money to be distributed among the poor of the parish—and ordered him to recompense Grimaldi for his torn shirt.

Old Lucas was outraged by the magistrate's decision and flatly refused to pay the fine. He was therefore swept off to the cells while Joseph was carried back, amidst general rejoicing, to renewed celebrations at the King of Prussia—where the question of who was to buy the next round was settled by the landlord's declaring that the drinks were on the house.

Grimaldi's Dormer

AFTER the death of his first wife, Maria, in October 1800, Joseph Grimaldi, in an effort to overcome his grief, moved to a new house in Baynes' Row.

The change of environment certainly helped, but as he was still prone to fits of despair whenever he was alone and unoccupied, he converted his attic into a 'dormer'—a sort of elaborate dovecote—and took to spending his leisure hours under the roof-tree breeding pigeons.

Besides distracting him and providing him with a great deal of pleasure, on one occasion those birds, or rather a particular bird, earned him a substantial amount of money. For he accepted a wager from a wealthy fancier named Lambert that none of his flock could fly twenty miles in under the same number of minutes. On the appointed day, despite adverse weather conditions, Grimaldi's pigeon completed the distance with a minute to spare, so winning him the sum of twenty pounds.

27

Grimaldi Burns his Leg and Gains a Wife

WHILE appearing at Sadler's Wells, in the summer of 1801, Joseph Grimaldi suffered a painful accident which led, indirectly, to his second marriage.

He was at the time portraying a bandit chieftain in a pantomime called *The Great Devil*. As he could scarcely hope to sustain such a part without being armed, he was provided with a pistol, which was concealed in one of his large black bandit chieftain's boots, and which he would withdraw and fire at a given moment in the performance. One evening, in the act of pulling the pistol from its hiding place, he accidently discharged it. The confined explosion caused the boot to balloon out to a preposterous size—to the delight of the audience, who assumed that the effect was intentional, and who laughed even louder when Grimaldi began hopping around the stage in a cloud of smoke.

For the person principally involved the accident was far from funny. Once he had recovered from the shock of the explosion he felt a searing pain in his leg, but, being in the middle of a scene and not wishing to disrupt it, he struggled manfully on in his part. When at last the scene was over and the boot removed, it was discovered that both his stocking and the wadding from the pistol—which had been primed, but not loaded —had been smouldering away, and that his foot was severely burnt.

As a result of this injury he was forced to take to his bed for five weeks: five weeks that would have been unendurable for him (since inactivity made him restless and miserable) had it not been for the visits of a pretty young actress from the Drury Lane Theatre named Mary Bristow. She called at his house every day; and by attending to his needs and his whims, by changing his bandages and plumping up his pillows, by preparing him trays and reading to him when his own eyes grew weary: by these and by innumerable other acts of kindness she rendered his enforced idleness if not pleasant then at least tolerable.

At the end of the five weeks his leg had healed and he was able to return to the stage. And the following Christmas Eve he married Mary Bristow, according to one source, 'in gratitude for her kindness'.

The Extraordinary Squire Mackintosh

THE SEASON at Sadler's Wells in 1804 was unusually demanding, and thus by the autumn—when the season came to an end—Joseph Grimaldi was thoroughly exhausted.

He happened to mention this one day in the course of a conversation with his childhood friend the Harlequin, Jack Bologna, who had also been engaged that year at Sadler's Wells; and as the latter remarked that he was not feeling too well himself, Grimaldi suggested that they should take a short holiday. Bologna agreed that a holiday was just what they needed, and moreover declared that he had an acquaintance, a country gentleman, who had often pressed him to come and stay at his seat in Kent. As this gentleman was very keen on the theatre, Bologna was sure that he would be more than willing to play host to Grimaldi as well, and he therefore proposed that the two of them should take advantage of his hospitality for a few days—unless, of course, Grimaldi had any objections.

Needless to say, Grimaldi had no objections; and a week later, Bologna having made all the necessary arrangements, they set off in a hired gig for Bromley, which was the nearest town to their destination.

Bologna used the opportunity that the journey provided to tell Grimaldi what he knew of their host, whose name, it emerged, was Mackintosh. He explained that although he had never visited him before, he had gathered from what Mackintosh had told him—which was borne out by the way he conducted himself whilst in London—that he was a man of private means, certainly not *in any way* connected with business or trade, and master not only of a large and comfortable house, but also of a great many acres of land: which acres, Bologna added with relish, were well stocked with game birds.

Grimaldi was delighted to hear that their holiday was to be spent in such congenial surroundings, and, being as keen a sportsman as his companion, that they were to have the chance of getting in some shooting. Indeed, he began to grow quite excited at the prospect of meeting Mackintosh, who was evidently a landowner of wealth and importance.

In the event this meeting took place rather sooner than either of the two occupants of the gig expected, for as they were approaching the outskirts of Bromley they were hailed by a man in a patched and threadbare jacket, who was sitting in a cart at the side of the road.

'It's me—Mackintosh,' the man shouted, waving and getting down from his cart. 'I've been waiting for you—I feared you might get lost.' Coming up to the gig, he extended his hand to Grimaldi, saying, 'Pleased to meet yer, Joey.'

Grimaldi was almost as confused by the great landowner's manner as he was by his workman-like appearance, neither of which struck him as being congruous with a man of his standing. However, he was reassured by his hand, which was, he noted, soft and white and most *un*workman-like, and since Bologna showed no sign of thinking that anything was amiss, Grimaldi refrained from making any comment.

The greetings over, Mackintosh returned to his vehicle and proceeded to lead the way to his house. But he would insist on stopping every few hundred yards in order to draw their attention to the local places of interest. Having thus passed slowly through the town, they finally drew up beside a small country inn, and Grimaldi and Bologna assumed rather wearily (for, in truth, they had had difficulty in sharing their host's enthusiasm for the sights of Bromley) that this was merely another old building that some famous person was supposed to have slept in. However, to their consternation Mackintosh pointed proudly to the inn and said, 'My home, gentlemen, and yours too, for as long as you care to stay.'

'Your home—a wayside tavern!' exclaimed Bologna reproachfully. 'But you told me … You told me you were a man of leisure.'

'And so I am,' returned Mackintosh chuckling, 'for Mother—whom you'll meet presently—runs things here, leaving me free to do just as I please.' He paused to wave to an old woman in an apron who at that moment appeared at a downstairs window, and then went on, 'As you know, Jack, I like to play the great man while I'm in London, and this—' he pointed to the inn again and lowered his voice—'is what you might call my little secret, which I reveal only to trusted friends like you and Joe. P'raps you expected something a little grander? But what difference does it make?—the food and beds here are the equal of any nobleman's.'

Mackintosh duly introduced his guests to Mother, who promptly sat them down to the huge feast that she had prepared in their honour. When at last they had eaten their fill, Bologna, who was by that time back on speaking terms with their host, broached the subject of shooting. Mackintosh encouraged the two actors by telling them that he had never known a year when there had been a greater abundance of game; and as it never occurred to either of them to doubt whether the surrounding land actually belonged to him, they made plans to commence their sport the following day.

But after spending an extremely comfortable night—for Mrs. Mackintosh's beds were indeed as soft and clean as any nobleman's—Grimaldi and Bologna awoke to find that a thick fog had descended, and that shooting was out of the question. They consoled themselves with the thought that it was bound to lift before the morrow, and passed the time very pleasantly, drinking and chatting with the customers in the bar and devouring the gargantuan meals that Mother continued to produce at regular intervals.

The next morning the fog had indeed lifted. As soon as breakfast was over, Mackintosh having armed his guests and provided them with a large sack, the hunting party sallied forth into the countryside. The two actors followed their host—who had decided at the last moment not to carry a gun—until he brought them to a halt close to a gate in a hedge, on the other side of which lay a field of buckwheat.

'There's usually plenty o' game feeding in there,' he said, nodding in the direction of the buckwheat; and leaving Grimaldi and Bologna to prepare their firearms he tiptoed up to the gate and peeped over. Mackintosh then motioned the two actors to join him. 'Birds—'undreds of 'em!'

'Birds?' ejaculated Bologna angrily, after he and Grimaldi had peered into the field. 'I don't call those birds. I call those pigeons.'

'Them's birds,' insisted Mackintosh. 'They've got wings, ain't they? They can fly, can't they? Them's birds all right.'

'You mean to say that you've brought us all this way to shoot pi —'

'Shhh, Jack—you'll frighten them away!' said Grimaldi, who was anxious to avoid any unpleasantness, adding in a whisper that, while he conceded that pigeons were inferior fare, it would be a pity if they were to return from their expedition empty-handed. With this observation Bologna wholeheartedly concurred, and straightaway he and Grimaldi raised their guns to their shoulders and fired into the flock of pigeons. There were, as Mackintosh had pointed out, literally hundreds of birds in the field, and since both actors were good marksmen, they succeeded in killing more than they could hope to carry.

'If that's the lot,' Mackintosh said, when Grimaldi and Bologna had finished tying up the neck of the sack, 'you'd better make a run for it.'

'Make a run for it?' laughed Bologna, glancing up at Mackintosh. 'Whatever for?'

''Cos if the Squire nabs you with that bundle he'll run you in for poaching.'

And without further ado Mackintosh made off, leaving his guests to find their own way back to the inn. Bologna was furious, and even went so far·as to suggest reloading their guns and going after him. But Grimaldi reasoned with his volatile friend, and by the time they reached the inn—which they managed to do without being intercepted by the Squire or his agents—he had succeeded, though not without difficulty, in persuading Bologna to take a more philosophical view of their adventure.

Mackintosh greeted them at his door as if nothing had happened. The two actors, who had previously resolved to leave for London as soon as they had returned his equipment, then espied Mother carrying a joint of beef into the dining room and decided to postpone their departure until after luncheon. This meal proved as agreeable as its predecessors, and thus when they finally took their leave of Mackintosh, they did so with considerably less formality than might otherwise have been expected.

The day after their return to London, Grimaldi and Bologna met by chance in Covent Garden and decided to go and talk over their curious holiday at the Garrick's Head, a public house in Bow Street run by a former actor. Upon entering the tavern they were greeted by Spencer, the proprietor, who, insisting that they join him over a bottle of wine, steered them into his private quarters; where, having made themselves comfortable, they treated him to a lively account of their Kentish escapade.

'Bless me! P-p-pigeons!' spluttered the publican, spilling the contents of his glass. 'If only you two had come to your ole chum Spencer and told 'im you wanted some sport! Why I was born an' bred in Kent, and I think I must know just about every gamekeeper in the county. I could 'ave arranged for you to take potshots at something better 'n pigeons. Talking of keepers ... ' Spencer broke off to welcome a man who had just then entered the room. 'Joseph—Joseph Clarke. What brings you to town, my friend, business or pleasure?'

'Squire's business I'm afraid, Spence,' replied the newcomer sitting down. 'Had a couple of Londoners down poaching his game. An' Squire's sent me up with a constable—'e's in the bar—to apprehend 'em.'

'Hmm. London's a big place yer know, Joe,' observed Spencer.

The gamekeeper agreed that it was considerably larger than Bromley, but went on to explain that a local man, a great theatre-goer, had seen the culprits and recognised them as being a Clown and a Harlequin employed at one of the London theatres. It was for this reason, he added, that he had sought Spencer out, hoping that, as an ex-actor, he might be able to help him track them down.

By this time it was of course quite plain to Grimaldi and Bologna that the two men the gamekeeper was after were none other than themselves; and they therefore nervously eyed the publican as he frowned and thoughtfully tugged at his whiskers, fearing that he might inadvertently give the game away.

But after a few seconds Spencer's frown disappeared, and he said to Clarke, 'Jus' supposin'—supposin' mind—that these 'ere actors of yours were specially good friends of mine … '

'Well, if that were the case, Spence,' replied the other slowly and looking rather doubtful, 'I'd natcherly not be so inclined to pursue the matter.'

'And supposin' these actors were not only friends of mine but also willing to pay a fair price for their sport *and* stand you a rumpsteak-an'-wine dinner.'

'Ah! Now you're talking!' said Clarke, his face lighting up. 'On those terms I certainly won't press the matter. An' yer can tell your friends that in return for the dinner they can come down to the 'state any time they like an' have some *real* shooting.'

'No need for me to do that, Joe!' exclaimed the publican triumphantly. 'You jus' told 'em yourself!'

And so, thanks to Spencer, everything was settled in an amicable fashion; and a few days later Grimaldi and Bologna revisited the Squire's estate, where, with the gamekeeper's assistance, they succeeded in bagging more than two dozen pheasants in less than two hours.

Fête-champêtre

Grimaldi and his friends
at a summer picnic

Grimaldi at Work

LONDON theatres in Joseph Grimaldi's time—unlike West End theatres today—were only open for part, usually less than half, of the year; and since the season varied from one theatre to another, it was not merely possible for a popular panto-mimist to be engaged on a regular basis at more than one theatre, it was, if he wished to secure a steady income for himself, a necessity. Thus throughout his working life Grimaldi was regularly em-ployed by two theatres: by Sadler's Wells and Drury Lane during his youth and early manhood, and subsequently, after he quarrelled with the manager of the latter theatre in 1806, by Sadler's Wells and Covent Garden.

However, the Sadler's Wells season at times coincided with those of the other two theatres, and when this was the case Grimaldi would often have to appear in two different productions in the same evening. As Drury Lane and Covent Garden were both situated nearly two miles away from the Wells, on those nights he was frequently only able to fulfil his com-mitments with great difficulty, and—especially when he was young and unable to afford the price of a cab—at the expenditure of a great deal of energy.

On one occasion, he and another actor named Bob Fairbrother, who was at that time, like Grimaldi, employed at both Sadler's Wells and Drury Lane, were detained at the former theatre beyond the usual time. Dis-covering when they were at last free to leave that there were but a few minutes left before they were expected on the stage at Drury Lane, they set off 'hand-in-hand' from Sadler's Wells and raced to the stage-door of Drury Lane in eight minutes.

On another occasion, young Grimaldi and the aforementioned Fair-brother ran, again through necessity, from Sadler's Wells to the Italian Opera House in the Haymarket (where the Drury Lane company were then appearing) in fourteen minutes—and would have covered the dis-tance even more quickly had not one or other, or both of them, had a collision with an old lady on the way. After Grimaldi had taken part in a procession (which was all that was expected of him), he sprinted back on his own to Sadler's Wells, where he immediately changed costume and, without taking a rest, took to the stage again—for the third time that evening.

No man, no matter how strong his constitution, and at the outset of his career Grimaldi certainly did possess a strong constitution, could hope to endure such exertions as these for any length of time and not pay a

price. There can be little doubt that the strain of working at two theatres at the same time, coupled with the rigours of his profession, helped to bring about that deterioration in Grimaldi's health which eventually forced him to quit the boards while he was yet a middle-aged man.

The Six Ladies and Six Gentlemen

SITTING quietly reading at his home in Baynes' Row one morning early in January 1807, Joseph Grimaldi was suddenly interrupted by his maidservant, who announced that there was someone to see him—a gentleman whom she did not recognise and who declined to give his name. Grimaldi bid the girl show the gentleman in and then, laying down his book, rather irritably checked his pockets to make sure he had some loose change. For, like many men who have achieved fame, he was constantly being bothered by callers, and in his experience it was usually impossible to get rid of the sort-who-declined-to-give-their-names unless he parted with a few pence.

However, the person that the maidservant ushered into the room was not seeking charity, nor indeed was he a stranger to Grimaldi: it was none other than Mackintosh, his old friend—if he can be deemed such—from Bromley. But he had changed so much since their last meeting that for a few seconds the Clown had difficulty in believing that it really was Mackintosh. His manners had greatly improved, he was smartly even fashionably dressed, and, it emerged in the course of the ensuing conversation, he had relinquished his life of idleness and was now engaged in some sort of business in London—Mother having sold the inn a few months previously and retired with the proceeds to another part of the country.

Now Grimaldi, although far from pleased at seeing Mackintosh again, was always disposed to think the best of his fellow men. And thus by the end of their interview he had persuaded himself that his visitor was a reformed character, and calling to mind the hospitable treatment that he and Jack Bologna had received while in Kent, he asked him to lunch the following Sunday.

Mackintosh proved to be an exemplary guest. He turned up punctually, told some very amusing anecdotes, admired the way Grimaldi carved the roast beef, complimented Mrs. Grimaldi on her cooking (it was the servants' day off), and generally behaved himself so well and was such good company that the couple invited him to dine with them again. His conduct at the second meal merely confirmed the good impression that he had created at the first: and, as the Grimaldis developed a liking for the man and a taste for his society, he soon became a regular visitor at their house.

One day, about a month after he had first appeared at Baynes' Row, Mackintosh dropped in on Grimaldi and told him that he had some friends

who were very anxious to make his acquaintance, and who therefore hoped that he would consent to dine with them at their house in Charlotte Street one night after he had finished at the theatre. At first Grimaldi shook his head and declared that it was out of the question: he had far too many commitments as it was, and what free evenings he had he wished to spend at home with his wife. Mackintosh, however, would not take no for an answer, and having succeeded in arousing Grimaldi's interest by representing his friends as influential people who might well be of service to him in his career, he eventually cajoled him into accepting their invitation and specifying a date.

On the appointed night, Grimaldi took a cab from the theatre to the address in Charlotte Street that Mackintosh had given him. But when he was deposited outside a large and brilliantly illuminated building, he assumed that there must have been some mistake—for it struck him as highly unlikely that Mackintosh could move in the same circles as the owners of such an imposing establishment. Nevertheless, reasoning that if it was the wrong house the doorman might at least be able to direct him to the right one, he knocked at the front door. To his surprise it was instantly opened by Mackintosh, who had evidently been awaiting his arrival, and who promptly demonstrated that he was indeed well acquainted with the owners of the establishment by introducing him to the host and hostess, Mr. and Mrs. Farmer. The Farmers in their turn introduced him to the five other couples who made up the company, and after the usual formalities Grimaldi, Mackintosh and the six ladies and six gentlemen all sat down to a magnificent supper.

Grimaldi was so overawed by the splendour of the surroundings in which he found himself and the elegance and sophistication of Mackintosh's friends that for the first few courses—and there were so many that he soon lost count of them—he felt awkward and out of place. The host and hostess, however, did their utmost to make him feel at home, and though he could hardly feel at home while dining off silver platters and being waited upon by liveried footmen, at length the combined influence of the Farmers' kindness and the excellent wine contrived to put him at his ease.

Once the meal was over and the cloth removed, the company commenced singing songs and telling stories. Needless to say, Grimaldi's contributions were much in demand, and as the six ladies and six gentlemen were obviously accustomed to keeping late hours, it was nigh on four o'clock in the morning before he was at last able to take his leave and make his way home. And if, when he got into bed, he did not immediately go to sleep, it was not for want of tiredness. For his wife, on hearing that he had spent the evening in such rich and fashionable society,

42

kept him awake for another whole hour plying him with questions—the majority of which, it might be added, concerned the cut and cloth of the six ladies' dresses.

Several days later Mackintosh called at Baynes' Row, and having established that Grimaldi had enjoyed himself at Charlotte Street, informed him that there was to be another party the following night, that the Farmers had invited the same five couples he had met a few nights previously, and that they hoped he would join them. Grimaldi, despite the fact that he really had enjoyed himself, responded to this invitation in much the same way as he had to the original one, and, on the grounds that he wished to spend the following evening with his wife, attempted to turn it down. But he was interrupted by Mackintosh, who said that he had foreseen the difficulty, that he had mentioned it to the Farmers, and that they had declared that fifteen were no more trouble to feed than fourteen, and that if Mrs. Grimaldi would care to accompany her husband, she would be as welcome at their house as he was.

This, as far as Grimaldi was concerned, settled the matter; and the following night he and his wife went to Charlotte Street.

Mrs. Grimaldi was dazzled by the splendour of the house and flattered by the attention that was paid to her by the six ladies and six gentlemen; and as she and Mrs. Farmer, finding that they had a common interest in fashion, immediately struck up a friendship, the latter led her to understand before they parted at the end of the evening that all future invitations would apply to her and her husband equally.

And there were many more invitations. For over the next two months, February and March, scarcely a week went by without Grimaldi and his wife dining at least once at Charlotte Street. The invitations were always brought by Mackintosh, the parties were always attended by the same six ladies and six gentlemen, and what with eating and drinking, and singing and story-telling, the festivities invariably extended into the early hours of the morning.

While Grimaldi continued to enjoy the parties, it gradually became apparent to him that there was something odd about them, or rather that there was something odd about the people whom he met at them—the six ladies and six gentlemen. For one thing, they were different from the other ladies and gentlemen he knew. And although he was unable to decide exactly what constituted the difference, he did notice that the six ladies' conversation was, for ladies, sometimes a trifle freer than perhaps it ought to have been, and that, for gentlemen, their six consorts wore an unusual number of rings and other items of jewellery. In addition, he was struck by the fact that the Farmers never invited any of their other friends—and he naturally supposed they had many—to their parties. For although, by the end of March, he and his wife had been to Charlotte Street upwards of a dozen times, the only people they ever met there were those who had been present on the occasion of his first visit.

But the thing that puzzled Grimaldi most of all about the six ladies and six gentlemen was their unwillingness to discuss or even reveal the origin of their wealth. They studiously avoided making any reference to the subject, and whenever he broached it they would either pretend not to hear or else adroitly steer the conversation in another direction. Mackintosh, who was himself far from explicit about the nature of the business he was engaged in, could not be prevailed upon to shed any light on the matter, which thus seemed to Grimaldi destined to remain for ever a mystery.

At the beginning of April, Mackintosh abruptly and inexplicably stopped calling at Baynes' Row, and for some time Grimaldi neither saw nor heard from him or the six ladies and six gentlemen. Then, after three weeks or thereabouts, he received a visit from a gentleman named Harmer.

'I, sir, am a lawyer,' commenced Mr. Harmer once he and Grimaldi were alone. And so saying he pulled a bundle of documents tied up with a length of pink silk ribbon from one of his pockets. 'An extremely busy one,' he continued, 'and as I do not intend to waste your time, I trust you will oblige me by not wasting mine. I have a number of questions to ask you. Your answers will be brief and to the point: the words I favour, sir, are "yes" and "no". Is that clear?'

Grimaldi nodded his head, and then, as the lawyer gave him a fierce look, quickly said, 'Yes.'

'Firstly, do you know a man called Mackintosh—or perhaps you know him by the name of Mackoul?'

'Mackintosh? Yes,' said Grimaldi.

'And did you know—and if you did not, Mr. Grimaldi, I must warn you that this may come as something of a shock to you—that he is, to put it bluntly, a criminal?'

'Mackintosh—a criminal? Good heavens, Mr. Harmer, it never—'

'No?' interjected the lawyer.

'No,' said the Clown.

Mr. Harmer then told Grimaldi that Mackintosh, alias Mackoul, had been arrested and charged with committing a burglary at Congleton in Cheshire on the night of the 13th March previous, and that he (Mr. Harmer) had been engaged to defend him. His purpose in calling on Grimaldi, he went on to explain, was to ascertain whether he could substantiate his client's alibi: for Mackintosh steadfastly maintained that he had not committed the burglary, claiming that, on the night in question,

45

he had been to see Grimaldi perform at a benefit at the Woolwich Theatre in London.

Grimaldi confirmed that he had indeed played at the Woolwich Theatre some time during the middle of March and that Mackintosh had been present, adding, after the lawyer had asked him whether he was positive that Mackintosh had been there, that he recalled the occasion very clearly: for Mackintosh and a dozen or so of his friends had taken a box that night and their splendid appearance had created quite a stir in the theatre. Although Grimaldi was unable to remember the exact date of the benefit, he managed to unearth an old theatrical bill advertising the event, which proved that it had taken place on the night of 13th March. Mr. Harmer took the poster into his possession, and having asked the Clown whether he would be prepared to repeat in court what he had told him, and having received a reply in the affirmative, he thrust his documents back in his pocket and bid him good day.

A few days later Mackintosh, having been released on bail, turned up at Baynes' Row. But for the fact that he wished to penetrate the mystery surrounding the six ladies and six gentlemen, Grimaldi would have sent the villain packing; instead the Clown received him with as much civility as his feelings would allow.

'There is one thing that baffles me,' said Grimaldi, when Mackintosh had finished thanking him for having agreed to appear in court on his behalf, 'and that is why you should choose to use me as a witness when you could call upon the testimony of your friends, the six ladies and six gentlemen. Surely, Mr. Mackintosh, *their* word would carry far more weight with a jury than mine?'

'They are no longer my friends!' exclaimed Mackintosh bitterly. 'And were they to put in an appearance at court my downfall would be ... '

Mackintosh never completed the sentence, for his voice trailed off and he fell silent, as if he had already said more than he intended. Grimaldi, however, demanded an explanation, and by degrees succeeded in dragging out of him the truth concerning the six ladies and six gentlemen.

In short, the reason why they were unlike other ladies and gentlemen, why they never invited strangers to their gatherings, and why they were so secretive about their occupations was that they were not really ladies and gentlemen at all but a gang of thieves and forgers. Mackintosh had fallen in with them upon his arrival in London, and had subsequently introduced Grimaldi to them at their insistence. For one day he had boasted to them that he knew Grimaldi, whereupon the gang, thinking that the Clown would make an amusing addition to their parties, had commenced badgering Mackintosh to bring him to Charlotte Street. This Mackintosh at length had agreed to do: Grimaldi's company had more than matched

46

up to their expectations, and Mackintosh had been obliged to promise that he would bring him again.

Latterly, however, the gang had turned against Mackintosh. For the burglary at Congleton had in fact been carried out by one of their number, a character by the name of Jones, who, Grimaldi suddenly remembered when Mackintosh came to mention it, had not been present at the Woolwich on the night of the benefit. Mackintosh had never been highly regarded at Charlotte Street, and thus when he had been arrested and charged with Jones's crime, the gang had closed ranks, and ever since they had been doing their utmost to ensure that he would be convicted in place of their comrade, whose guilt Mackintosh was unable to prove.

Grimaldi listened to Mackintosh's confession with a mixture of pity and anger: pity, because he could not but feel sorry for a man who, abandoned by the only people he had hitherto been able to call his friends, was now in grave danger of losing his life for a crime that he had not committed. But, in the end, it was Grimaldi's anger that prevailed. For in winding up his confession, Mackintosh happened to reveal that the six ladies and six gentlemen were *not married*; upon hearing which, Grimaldi, for whom this was the final straw, flew into a terrible rage. One would not like to conjecture what might have happened to Mackintosh had he not, 'with much wisdom', chosen that moment to effect his departure.

*   *   *

The following August Mackintosh stood trial at Stafford, where, largely as a result of Grimaldi's testimony and the corroboratory evidence of a theatrical bill dated 13th March, he was acquitted. The two men's paths never crossed again.

The Clown Bradbury

MONG Joseph Grimaldi's contemporaries and—for a brief period—rivals was a pantomimist named Bob Bradbury, who was known as the 'Brummel of Clowns'. He had earned this sobriquet by cultivating the society of the rich and titled and aping, as far as his resources permitted, their fashions and extravagances. He dressed like a dandy, kept a tame bear, and even possessed his own carriage—in short, he was one of those artists whose private lives are more often discussed than their talents.

Grimaldi was barely acquainted with this Clown, and he was therefore surprised, one morning in 1807, to receive a letter from him. Upon opening the letter, his surprise turned to alarm. Bradbury requested—after covering over half a sheet expressing his concern for the recipient's health, wealth, career and family—that he pay him a visit on a specified day; but it was not so much the contents of the letter that alarmed Grimaldi as the fact that it had been sent from a private lunatic asylum at Hoxton, then a small village north of London.

Now Grimaldi, like many people, even today, was frightened by madness, and wary of those afflicted with it. Thus, although he felt pity for the Clown, whom he quite naturally assumed had gone mad, and was inclined to comply with his request, at the same time he could not help suspecting that the familiar tone of the letter masked some dark and sinister motive. The more he read the letter, the more agitated he became, until eventually he worked himself up into such a state over it, and was so uncertain as to how he should respond to it, that he decided he needed the benefit of another's advice.

Accordingly he sought out a friend of his, a sensible well-balanced fellow named Lawrence, who suggested, once he had examined the letter and listened to Grimaldi's fears, that they visit the asylum together, reasoning that the two of them would be capable of overpowering Bradbury in the event of his becoming violent. Grimaldi was cheered by this proposal and accepted it; and a few days later he and his friend travelled to Hoxton.

They knocked on the stout door of the asylum, and gained admittance. Grimaldi introduced himself, and was rather taken aback when the old doorman responded by giving Lawrence a wink and saying, 'Joseph Grimaldi, eh? Ha, ha! Al'ays had plenty of Christs, and Napoleon's very allamode, but Grimaldi—that's a new one, eh sir? Ha, ha!'

Lawrence quickly cleared up this little misunderstanding, and secured

the services of a broad-shouldered individual who seemed to combine the offices of doctor and warder. He led them through the labyrinthine corridors of the institution, finally ushering them into the room that contained Bradbury.

Grimaldi was startled by Bradbury's appearance when he first saw him, and indeed hardly recognised him, for, as was the custom in asylums at that time, his head had been shaved and he was confined in a straitjacket. In order to hide his discomfort, Grimaldi attempted to strike up a conversation with the Clown. But he adopted, unconsciously, the soothing tone of voice and peculiar diction that adults who have no rapport with children invariably employ when speaking to them—with the result that Bradbury burst out laughing. Not perceiving the cause of his laughter, and assuming that the poor fellow had not understood what he said, Grimaldi started to repeat his remark, only to be interrupted by Bradbury, who protested that he was not mad. At this the two friends exchanged glances and shook their heads sadly. Bradbury was evidently a hopeless case: he was not merely mad, he was mad and he did not even know it!

Divining his visitors' thoughts, Bradbury decided that there was only one way to establish his sanity. He therefore asked them to sit down, and once they had done so, he gave them the following explanation of how he came to be in the asylum: or rather the following is a shortened version of the explanation he gave them, as his own account was too long and involved to be recorded here in full.

It had all started several months previously, when, at the end of an evening he had spent with a party of his aristocratic friends, he discovered that his snuff box had been stolen. The circumstances in which it disappeared led him to suspect that the culprit was a young nobleman who had been present at the party, and he was therefore disposed at first to interpret the theft as a joke. But when it became apparent that the young man in question had no intention of returning the snuff box, which was made of gold and extremely valuable, Bradbury obtained a warrant and had him arrested. The missing article was found in his possession, and as Bradbury was determined to prosecute, the thief was charged and committed for trial.

The young nobleman's relatives soon came to hear of his plight. In an effort to preserve the good name of the family, they tried to persuade Bradbury to abandon his action by offering him large sums of money. At first they were unable to tempt him; but he eventually gave way and agreed to co-operate with them in return for a substantial pension, which they undertook to pay him every year for the rest of his life.

By that time, however, it was too late for Bradbury simply to withdraw his charge, and he was faced with the problem of securing the thief's acquittal without arousing the suspicion of the law. After giving the matter some thought, he came up with an ingenious solution. He began to behave as if he had suddenly gone insane. After a suitable lapse of time, he caused himself to be committed to Hoxton asylum, arranging this in such a way that it appeared as if he was carried off against his will.

Thus when the trial was held a few weeks later, he was, apparently through no fault of his own, unable to attend, and the young nobleman was acquitted for lack of evidence. Shortly afterwards Bradbury ceased his pretence of madness and, having convinced his keepers that his recovery was permanent, obtained permission for his release. In fact he was due to leave on the following day.

Bradbury reached the end of his story and, having satisfied himself that he had succeeded in dispelling his visitors' apprehensions, went on to reveal why he had requested this meeting with Grimaldi. In a week's time a benefit was to be held for him at the Surrey Theatre: would Grimaldi, he wondered, be kind enough to participate, for he granted that Grimaldi's following was larger than his own, and his presence would therefore guarantee that the evening drew a large crowd.

Grimaldi instantly agreed to Bradbury's request, assuring him that nothing would give him greater pleasure. This matter having been settled, the conversation turned to other topics; and Bradbury's company proved to be so diverting that both Grimaldi and his friend were rather disappointed when their broad-shouldered guide returned, and announced that it was time for them to leave.

On the appointed night the benefit took place. Grimaldi sang and danced and did everything he could to ensure that the evening was a success—even helping beforehand to sell tickets at the door. All went well until about half-way through Bradbury's act, when, without any warning, he suddenly did something that was so obscene that the onlookers were shocked and disgusted. After the initial uproar had subsided, he defiantly did whatever it was again. The audience rose to their feet and expressed their indignation with such vehemence that he was forced for his own safety to flee the stage.

Bradbury had cause to regret this evening for the rest of his life. For word of his indecent behaviour quickly spread, and as a consequence he was prevented for many years from appearing at any of the London theatres. And although he managed to obtain occasional employment in the provinces, he never succeeded in re-establishing the reputation he had enjoyed prior to his sojourn in the lunatic asylum. At first his pension saved him from financial difficulty; but it seems that later he lost even this source of income: for when he died in 1831, Bob Bradbury died a pauper.

Hamilton the Jeweller

N 1808 Joseph Grimaldi was engaged as usual for the summer season at Sadler's Wells: a theatre which at that time differed from other London playhouses in so far as the management frequently arranged their programme so that the pantomime commenced, rather than concluded, the evening's entertainment. Whenever this was the case Grimaldi would find himself released from his duties at an unusually early hour; and since he enjoyed, in moderation, the pleasures of a good public house, on these nights he would call in at the Sir Hugh Myddleton —a popular local tavern. However, as his wife Mary was accustomed to wait up for him in Finchley (where he and his family spent the warmer months of the year), he rarely stayed for more than half an hour.

Among those whom he came to know in the course of his visits to the Sir Hugh was a young jeweller named George Hamilton, whose affected behaviour set him apart from the other regular customers. For Hamilton had, as they used to say, airs above his station: and despite the fact that he was a skilled craftsman and earned good wages, he despised his trade, never referred to it, and attempted to pass himself off as a gentleman. To this end he adopted a variety of absurd mannerisms, and, in the mistaken belief that generosity was an upper-class attribute, spent far more money than he could reasonably afford treating his fellow drinkers. However, he was, notwithstanding his faults, a likable man, and from time to time Grimaldi felt inclined to point out to him the foolishness of his affectations. Yet, knowing from experience that advice from acquaintances is liable to be interpreted as criticism, he always resisted the temptation to interfere.

There was one other peculiarity that Grimaldi noted about Hamilton: the third finger on his left hand was missing. And because he was unable to move the adjacent little finger, which remained permanently curled into his palm, a casual observer might well have supposed that the jeweller had only three digits on this hand. But then a casual observer would probably have missed Hamilton's deformity altogether. For he habitually concealed his left hand in his pocket, and only withdrew it on occasions when the use of both hands was required, or when he forgot himself, as he sometimes did when he was greatly excited or agitated.

The summer season at Sadler's Wells duly came to an end, and Grimaldi's engagements took him elsewhere. It was therefore not until Easter 1809, when the theatre opened again, that he was able to resume his visits to the Sir Hugh. Hamilton was still frequenting the house, and was now married to a pretty, kind-hearted girl, who often accompanied him there in the evenings. But, despite his marriage, he was no more reconciled to his lot in life than he had been before. Indeed, there was now a recklessness about his behaviour which at times led Grimaldi to think that he might be losing his grip upon himself. His moods fluctuated violently, his speech was sometimes wild and incoherent, he spent his money more extravagantly than ever, and, to make matters worse, he had taken to drinking heavily. Grimaldi also noticed that his taste in clothes, which had previously been sober and unremarkable, was now decidedly raffish.

The older customers partially attributed Hamilton's decline to the bad influence of Archer—a shifty, surly lout whom the jeweller had somehow fallen in with since the previous autumn. Although Grimaldi respected the opinion of the tavern's elders, he could at first find little to hold against the man beyond his disagreeable manner. But as time went by he observed that Hamilton was more frequently and more excessively intoxicated when in Archer's company, and finally he witnessed a scene

one night which left him in no doubt as to his despicable character.

On the night in question Hamilton, his wife and Archer arrived at the public house together. They sat down at a table, and Hamilton, who was already drunk, called out for a glass of gin, but before the pot-boy had had time to serve him, he fell forward on to the table in a stupor. Archer watched the jeweller for a few minutes and having satisfied himself that he was completely insensible, turned to his wife and indicated, by sneering and pointing at the body that was slumped between them, that he thought her husband a fool. He then leered at her and stretching over Hamilton's back, suddenly grabbed her hand and proceeded to squeeze it in an unmistakably amorous fashion. As soon as the poor girl realised what was happening she snatched her hand away and turned her back on him, obviously frightened and disgusted by his advances. Shortly afterwards Hamilton awoke. He gulped down his drink, and the three of them left the tavern.

The next evening Grimaldi was sitting quietly by himself in the Sir Hugh reading a newspaper when Hamilton, for once apparently sober, came over and politely asked if he might join him. They exchanged pleasantries and then Hamilton casually enquired how often he travelled back to Finchley to be with his family. Surprised and pleased by the jeweller's civility, Grimaldi put down his newspaper and explained that he usually went home every night, but that on that particular evening, having an engagement at his house in town, he would not be doing so. The following evening, however, he intended to go back to his family. Grimaldi having imparted this information, Hamilton steered the conversation on to other topics, and then got up and rejoined his wife at the bar.

The next day a party of Grimaldi's friends arrived unexpectedly from the country and he was obliged in consequence to spend two further nights in town. It was therefore not until three days after his conversation with Hamilton that he was at last free to return to Finchley. Before setting off in his gig he dropped in at the Sir Hugh, but as he was looking forward to seeing his family again he did not stay for long. Noticing that the jeweller was not there, he asked after him while he was paying for his drink, and was surprised to hear that he had not been seen that evening, nor, for that matter, for the previous two.

However, the time that Grimaldi had gained by leaving the public house early he more than lost a little later in his journey. A call that he had to make in Tottenham Court Road detained him longer than he had expected; then, passing through Kentish Town he was hailed by an old friend who insisted that he come into his house for a glass of wine. It was nearly midnight before he was back on the road to Finchley.

54

The sky was clear and the moon was bright, and as the pony was familiar with the route, Grimaldi allowed himself to succumb to the influence of the wine, and nodded off to sleep. He had travelled as far as Highgate Hill when the familiar swaying of the gig abruptly ceased. Sensing that the pony had stopped, he leaned forward dreamily to give the animal some word of encouragement—and at that moment was startled from his sleep by a stern cry of, 'Stand and deliver!'

He opened his eyes to find himself confronted by three masked and armed highwaymen. One—apparently the leader—was holding the pony by the bridle, while the other two were stationed on either side of his gig.

'Your money and your possessions,' barked the man holding the bridle. 'And no nonsense!' And to give emphasis to his last command he levelled his pistol at the trembling Clown.

'Tom, you take it from him,' he ordered, indicating with a flick of his pistol the man on Grimaldi's left.

Grimaldi handed over his cash to the highwayman called Tom, who stuffed it away in his greatcoat and then demanded his pocket watch as well. In spite of his fear, Grimaldi protested that the watch had little value, but as it had his portrait painted on the dial he was loath to part with it. His pleas were in vain, and Tom wrested the watch from him.

'You wouldn't treat me like this if you knew who I was,' the Clown complained.

'Oh, we *know* you all right, Grimaldi,' replied the leader. 'Why, we have spent the last three nights waiting just for you.'

Tom, who had been examining the watch, was about to put it away with the money when the third highwayman, who had until then been silent, spoke up on Grimaldi's behalf. 'Give it back, Tom—the gentleman's attached to it.' Then as an afterthought he added, 'Besides, the likeness will make it easy to trace.'

The two robbers began arguing as to whether or not they should keep the watch, and as they were doing so it struck Grimaldi that there was something familiar about the voice of the man on his right. In the end the leader cut short the dispute by ordering Tom to return the watch, and since he hesitated, the third highwayman went round the gig, took it from him and thrust it back at Grimaldi: who noticed that the hand that pushed the watch into his was missing—or seemed to be missing—two fingers.

A moment later the highwaymen disappeared and Grimaldi, who had been frightened and confused by the ordeal, was suddenly seized by an irrational desire to flee from the scene of the robbery. He leapt down from the gig and started running up the road in the direction in which he had

been travelling. He had not got very far when he literally ran into the night patrol responsible for that stretch of the highway. The officer caught hold of Grimaldi, who, once he had regained his breath and his faculties, explained what had happened to him.

When the Clown had finished his somewhat muddled account the night patrol announced that he was confident that he knew who the highwaymen were, for he had observed three men lurking in the vicinity for the past three nights. As he was equally confident that he would be able to arrest them before daybreak, he told Grimaldi that he was to come at twelve o'clock the following day to Bow Street, where it would be necessary for him to identify the men so that they could be committed for trial. He then saw Grimaldi safely back to his vehicle and hurried off in pursuit of the three highwaymen.

Although Grimaldi was exhausted when he finally crawled into his bed in Finchley, he was unable to sleep. He tossed and turned, troubled by the prospect of the visit he would have to make to Bow Street. For he was certain that Hamilton would be among those apprehended by the night patrol, and, knowing how severe the penalties were for those convicted of highway robbery, it appalled him to think how his evidence might ruin the young lives of the jeweller—who was after all more misguided than wicked—and the kind-hearted creature he had made his wife. Debating with himself as to whether or not he should testify against the robbers, he lay awake until well after cock-crow.

Later that same morning Grimaldi was met by the night patrol and a magistrate at Bow Street. The night patrol was obviously pleased with himself. He had caught his suspects and, although none of the stolen money had been found on them, he was *sure* Mr. Grimaldi would have no difficulty in identifying them. Grimaldi was led downstairs and shown into a cell containing the three prisoners. Two of them were unknown to him but, as he had feared, he *was* acquainted with the third.

'Good heavens—Joey Grimaldi!' Hamilton exclaimed, as Grimaldi entered the dingy room, and then indicating his surroundings he added, 'As you can see there's been the most terrible mistake.'

'You know this man?' the night patrol enquired.

Grimaldi agreed that he did.

But Grimaldi was too experienced an actor to be taken in by Hamilton's display of innocence: and when the two officials were distracted for a few seconds by the blaspheming of one of the other prisoners, he looked the jeweller straight in the eye and, holding up his left hand, turned down two fingers.

At once Hamilton realised the game was up: the muscles in his carefully composed face suddenly stiffened, and his left leg began to shake uncontrollably. He opened his mouth as if to say something, but Grimaldi turned away.

'Well, sir. Do you recognise all or any of them?' demanded the night patrol.

Grimaldi shook his head by way of reply.

'Are you sure?' the night patrol persisted.

'Certain.'

The two officials did not hide their disappointment: the prisoners could not be convicted on circumstantial evidence alone.

Eventually, and only after he had persuaded the magistrate and the night patrol that he was neither tired nor concussed and that it would be pointless for him to return the next day as he would be no better able to identify the suspects, Grimaldi was allowed to go, knowing that Hamilton and his accomplices would be freed later that afternoon.

A few days afterwards Hamilton paid Grimaldi a visit in Finchley. Although it would be exaggerating to say that the jeweller had been transformed by his experiences, he was certainly a humbled and chastened man. As soon as he and Grimaldi were alone in the parlour, he fell on his knees and, sobbing with remorse and gratitude, begged to be forgiven. Grimaldi perceived that his repentance was genuine, but he agreed to forgive him only on the condition that he gave his word to devote himself henceforth to his wife and his trade. This Hamilton willingly did, whereupon Grimaldi, seeing that he was plainly uncomfortable, raised him from his knees and seated him in an armchair. Hamilton then explained how he and the others had been led astray by Archer; how it had been Archer who had planned the crime without taking part in it; and how Archer had met them immediately after the robbery and taken Grimaldi's money into 'safe-keeping', and had since disappeared.

Several weeks later, the doorkeeper at Sadler's Wells brought Grimaldi a package which had been left with him by a soberly dressed gentleman who had deemed it unnecessary to leave his name. The package contained the exact amount of money that the Clown had lost in the robbery.

Grimaldi and Lord Byron

JOSEPH GRIMALDI discovered towards the end of October in the year 1812 that his services were temporarily not required at either Sadler's Wells or Covent Garden. There being nothing else to detain him in London, he travelled to Cheltenham and there performed with great success for two nights at a theatre belonging to a man named Watson.

On the last night Watson, delighted by the returns, persuaded him to undertake two further engagements at Gloucester, where he also owned a theatre. The next day they therefore went to that town, and secured rooms at an inn; and in the evening Grimaldi played once again to a packed house.

At the end of the pantomime, in accordance with the practice that they had established in Cheltenham, Grimaldi and his employer dined together. Once the dishes had been cleared away, Grimaldi, assuming that they were going to sit up drinking and talking until the early hours (as they had done on the two previous occasions), asked the waiter to bring them a large bowl of punch. But when the punch arrived Watson advised him to limit himself to a single glass of the beverage, explaining that they would have to rise early the following morning.

Grimaldi took a sip of the punch and, finding it excellent, questioned whether it was really necessary for them to rise early.

'Indeed it is,' replied Watson severely. 'I saw Colonel Berkeley at the theatre this evening, and he invited you and me to join him and a party of his friends for a morning's hare coursing at Berkeley Castle. Naturally I accepted.'

'Naturally,' said Grimaldi, who had yet to hear of a commoner turning down an invitation from a member of the aristocracy. He then asked Watson what time he meant by 'early'. And on learning that as they were expected for breakfast they would have to depart before dawn, he promptly drained his glass and retired to bed.

The next morning the two men travelled in a chaise to Berkeley Castle. Their host greeted them upon their arrival with great condescension; and after informing them that breakfast was about to be served, proceeded to introduce them to such of their fellow guests as they did not already know—one of whom was Lord Byron.

It so happened that the great poet was in a capricious mood that morning, and thus when it came to his turn to have Grimaldi introduced to him, he decided—as he intimated to the Lady with whom he had been flirting—that he would have some fun at the Clown's expense. Accordingly he approached him in a most servile manner, executed a number of impertinent bows, and then made a short but absurdly eloquent speech, praising the actor's talents and expressing his delight at making his acquaintance.

At first Grimaldi was baffled by Byron's behaviour. Indeed, such was the simplicity of his character, it is doubtful whether he would have realised that he had been mocked had it not been for the ill-suppressed giggles of some of the younger ladies present. But once he had perceived the peer's intention he was determined to retaliate. Constrained, however, by the other man's superior rank, he reluctantly contented himself with returning all his bows, adding a few more of his own for good measure.

He then glanced at Colonel Berkeley and, catching his eye, pulled a face, which, though it was merely intended to convey his discomfort, was so extraordinary that all those who caught sight of it burst out laughing. Byron, who had not seen Grimaldi's expression, looked round in vain for the cause of the laughter, thereby setting it off all over again, and stalked back to his place at the side of Lady ———, uncertain as to who had got the better of whom.

After breakfast all the gentlemen, excepting those laid up with gout, and a languid young man who maintained that hare coursing was cruel and barbaric, ventured out into the fields with the dogs. However, out of consideration for all those who share the languid young man's views, we will not dwell on that part of the day's proceedings and, without even revealing whether Grimaldi enjoyed himself or not, rejoin him and the rest of the company at half past eleven, when they assembled in the main dining room for luncheon—the Colonel having brought forward the meal so as to enable his two theatrical guests to partake of it prior to their departure.

At the dining table Grimaldi found himself seated with Lord Byron on his right, and another nobleman, with whom he had a slight acquaintance, on his left. Grimaldi and the nobleman enquired after each other's health, and then, while the first course was being served, the latter leant towards the Clown and asked him in a whisper whether he knew Byron.

'No,' replied Grimaldi. 'No, I can't claim that I do. For although I have frequently seen him in the green-rooms of the theatres in town, I have never actually conversed with him.'

'In that case,' said the nobleman, drawing even closer to Grimaldi, and winking at Byron, 'perhaps I should warn you of one of His Lordship's little eccentricities. Whenever he dines in company it is his custom to offer food and drink to his neighbours: quite why he does this I do not know—but I *do* know that he takes great offence if his offerings are declined. Obviously a man in your precarious profession would have no wish to fall out with someone of Byron's status and influence; and I therefore suggest that if he presses you to take anything—as he undoubtedly will—that you accept it.'

Grimaldi cheerfully thanked the nobleman for his advice; and, having selected what he hoped were the correct knife and fork from the bewildering array of cutlery that lay before him on the table, turned his attention to his food. No sooner had he finished what was on his plate than Byron suggested that he might like some more. Grimaldi, of course, agreed that he would. And from that moment onwards he was kept so busy eating and drinking all the things that Byron prescribed that he scarcely had time to speak. Thus, by the time the dessert was served—it was apple pie—he had eaten such a vast quantity of food that he seriously began to doubt whether he would be capable of performing in the evening; however, as he was inordinately fond of apple pie, he allowed Byron to cut him a slice.

'Now that I've ... ' chuckled Byron, turning to Lady ———, who had been sitting all this time on his right, feeling rather neglected, 'Now that I've filled him up, I think it's time to administer an emetic.' Turning back to Grimaldi, who was about to start on his pudding, he exclaimed with apparent surprise, 'Why, Mr. Grimaldi, do you not take soy sauce with your pie?'

Grimaldi replied that though the combination sounded unusual he was willing to experiment, and accepting a bottle of the sauce from Byron, shook it liberally over his apple pie. After sampling one or two spoonfuls of the ruined pudding, he pushed his bowl to one side. Whereupon, recalling the nobleman's advice, and fearing that Byron might take offence, he turned to him and declared that though he had hitherto eaten all the good things that His Lordship recommended, he found that the combination of soy and pie was not to his taste, and therefore hoped that His Lordship would forgive him if he left what remained in his bowl.

Byron, who was not altogether a heartless man, was touched by Grimaldi's apology, and deciding that the Clown had endured enough, pronounced him a good fellow and clapped him heartily on the back— which, in view of the condition of Grimaldi's stomach, almost had disastrous consequences.

Directly the meal was over, Grimaldi and Watson thanked and took leave of their host, and, after a slight delay caused by the difficulty the former experienced in climbing into the chaise (a feat which, had it not been for the assistance of two burly footmen, he might never have accomplished), drove back to Gloucester.

61

Despite the unpropitious nature of their first meeting, Grimaldi and Byron subsequently became firm friends. Grimaldi, however, never lost his awe of the poet; and as the latter was capable, when vexed, of saying the most unkind and hurtful things, Grimaldi always made a point of sounding out his views on a particular subject before expressing an opinion himself. For his part, Byron invariably treated Grimaldi with great kindness. And before he left England 'upon the expedition whence he was destined to return no more', he demonstrated his regard for him by presenting him with what afterwards became the Clown's most treasured possession: a valuable silver snuff box, bearing the inscription: 'The gift of Lord Byron to Joseph Grimaldi'.

Byron's death in 1824 doubtless saddened Grimaldi, who, as I have recorded elsewhere, quit the stage the previous year in poor health. Grimaldi outlasted his noble friend by thirteen less than happy years. In 1837, by that time infirm and incapable of walking, he was accustomed to spending his evenings in the Marquis of Cornwallis, a tavern situated a few doors away from his house, and which he was able to visit with the help of the landlord, who would carry him to and fro on his back. At about a quarter to eleven on the night of Tuesday 31st May, he parted from the landlord saying, 'God bless you, my boy. I shall be ready for you tomorrow night.' He was not; for the next morning his housekeeper, on attempting to awake him, found that he was dead.

He was buried the following Monday in the graveyard of St. James's Chapel, Pentonville, where his gravestone may still be seen today.

POSTSCRIPT. The 'incidents' described in the preceding pages have all been adapted from the *Memoirs of Joseph Grimaldi*, an edited version of the Clown's autobiography which first appeared nine months after his death, in 1838. Prior to publication Grimaldi's manuscript had in fact been edited twice: first by a journalist he himself had engaged, and subsequently by no less a person than Charles Dickens, or 'Boz' as he signed himself at that stage of his literary career. Strictly speaking, however, Dickens did more than edit the *Memoirs*, for he rewrote Grimaldi's already revised and abridged manuscript from beginning to end in the third person—thereby transforming it into a biography. Yet Dickens was not by temperament a biographer, and since he concentrated on retelling 'in a more attractive manner' what he deemed to be the most interesting episodes in the manuscript, the result of his labours was an anecdotal account of Grimaldi's life, distinguished more for its liveliness and readability than for its veracity.

In turn, I have allowed myself a certain amount of freedom in relating the 'incidents' contained in the present volume in order to complement my mother's paintings. Those readers who wish to learn more about Grimaldi or the pantomime tradition to which he both belonged and contributed should read either the *Memoirs* themselves, which have been reprinted many times since 1838, most recently in 1968 by MacGibbon & Kee, with corrections by Richard Findlater, or else *Joe Grimaldi, His Life and Theatre* (Cambridge University Press, 1978), a biography, also by Richard Findlater, to whose research I here acknowledge my debt.